The
SHADOW-WORK
JOURNAL

*A guided journal to help you
navigate, integrate, and transcend
your shadow.*

WE'RE HERE BECAUSE OF YOU.

When you're supporting our business, you're supporting a dream.

Share a picture or video of your journal on TikTok or Instagram for **20% OFF your next purchase!**

DM @zenfulnote or email keila@zenfulnote.com with your video link to receive your special discount.

Let's vibe!

Learn about The 369 Method, Manifesting Techniques, Shadow Work, and more. Follow our @zenfulnote social channels.

DECLARATION OF INTENT

I,_____, vow on this day to commit to my personal growth and acceptance. I promise to fill this journal out with an open heart and good intentions. I acknowledge that there are both pure and wounded parts to my being, and I choose to embrace and nurture both. I look forward to unveiling my shadows and bringing more light into this world through my personal journey of self-reflection and healing.

_____

SIGNATURE

_____

START DATE

_____

COMPLETION DATE

CONTENTS

1. ABOUT SHADOW WORK

2. SHADOW WORK EXERCISES

3. SHADOW WORK JOURNAL PROMPTS

4. GETTING TO THE ROOT

1

SHADOW WORK
INTRODUCTION

UNLESS YOU LEARN TO FACE
YOUR OWN SHADOWS, YOU
WILL CONTINUE TO SEE THEM IN
OTHERS, BECAUSE THE WORLD
OUTSIDE OF YOU IS ONLY A
REFLECTION OF THE WORLD
INSIDE OF YOU.

CARL JUNG

What is shadow work?

Shadow work is about revealing the unknown. The shadow is an unconscious aspect of your personality that the ego does not identify with. You may experience your shadow when you're triggered in social interactions, relationships, in episodes of anxiety or sadness.

The unconscious mind contains repressed emotions from painful events, causing impulsive behaviors and unwanted patterns that form your "dark side". In short, the shadow is composed of the parts of yourself that you have forgotten, abandoned, and repressed in order to grow and fit in with the mold of society. Think back to your childhood and recall the ways in which you would express yourself only to be rejected. You may have been crying and told to stop. You may have been laughing uncontrollably in a classroom and given a dirty glance from your teacher or peers.

There are countless ways in which you may have been reprimanded for what was deemed as "bad" and praised for what was "good" - learning to adjust your behavior accordingly. These repressed parts of yourself don't go away forever. They are stored and locked inside your unconscious mind. Shadow Work is the process of revealing, accepting, and integrating these parts of yourself that you have repressed and rejected. The techniques in **The Shadow Work Journal** will allow you to dive into unconscious pockets of repressed emotions and transcend the negative effects they currently have on your well-being.

The goal is to make the unconscious conscious so that you may work on them in self-reflection and acceptance. While anyone can do shadow work, a licensed mental health expert is a good option, especially for individuals who have experienced severe trauma or abuse.

Before beginning your shadow work, it is important to set an intention to openly notice and question your own reactions. The shadow is apparent in strong emotions and dissatisfaction. Be sure to keep a mental log of these sensations to truly understand where patterns occur, and use this journal as a tool to identify what is causing them. The **"get to the root" pages** are an excellent resource to track your shadows and their roots.

Why Shadow Work is Important

There are many benefits to shadow work. Your pains and triggers can be guides to help you understand what you deeply care about, bringing you closer to your life purpose. Conversely, you will come to identify toxic patterns in your life and change them completely.

Another benefit of shadow work is that you will develop more courage and confidence to face the unknown and **embody your whole self.**

You will develop deeper love, acceptance, and understanding of yourself, which helps improve your relationships with others. Practicing shadow work helps you separate from egotistical thoughts and will increase empathy and compassion for others. Compassion in turn helps exercise other forms of positive emotions like gratitude that can better your mental and psychical health.

Failure to face and deal with the shadow elements can be the seed of adversities and prejudice between unrepresented groups or individuals, and can trigger anything from a small argument to a major war. Recognizing shadow elements is an integral part of becoming a compassionate and reasonable individual.

The Father of Shadow Work: Carl Jung

The concept of the shadow was first developed by Swiss psychiatrist and psychoanalyst Carl Jung. Jung believed that exploring the shadow was essential for personal growth and individuation, the process of becoming one's authentic self. The shadow refers to the unconscious parts of our psyche that contain our repressed thoughts, feelings, and impulses. It is the side of ourselves that we reject or hide from others, and often from ourselves. However, these repressed aspects of ourselves can still influence our behavior and emotional states.

Understanding the Psyche

The psyche is a term used to describe the inner world of our thoughts, feelings, and emotions. It is the source of our experiences, motivations, and behaviors, and it is constantly evolving and changing throughout our lives. Understanding the psyche is key to understanding ourselves and the world around us.

Jung believed that the psyche was composed of several distinct but interrelated parts, including the conscious mind, the unconscious mind, the personal unconscious, and the collective unconscious.

The conscious mind is the part of our psyche that is aware of our thoughts and experiences. The unconscious mind contains thoughts, feelings, and experiences that are outside our conscious awareness. The personal unconscious is the part of the psyche that contains repressed thoughts, feelings, and experiences, while the collective unconscious is the part of the psyche that contains archetypes, universal symbols and themes that are shared by all people. One of the key benefits of understanding the psyche is increased self-awareness. When we have a greater understanding of our thoughts, feelings, and emotions, we can make more conscious choices, improve our relationships with others, reduce anxiety and emotional distress.

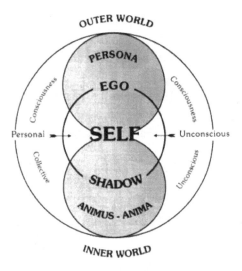

Figure 1; Jung's model of the Psyche

Jung believed that exploring the psyche was essential for personal growth and individuation, the process of becoming one's authentic self. He believed that by exploring the unconscious mind, we could gain a deeper understanding of our motivations, reactions, and behaviors, and make changes to live more authentic lives. Jung's theories have been highly influential in the field of psychology and have been further developed by other psychoanalytic theorists, including Sigmund Freud and Melanie Klein. Today, the study of the psyche is an interdisciplinary field that draws on psychology, neuroscience, philosophy, and spirituality.

"The meeting of two personalities is like the contact of two chemical substances: if there is any reaction, both are transformed."

-CARL JUNG

MIND TRAPS

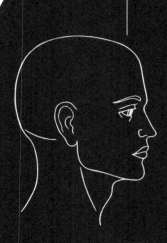

ANCHORING
The 1st thing you judge influences your judgement of all that follows.

CONFIRMATION BIAS
You favor things that confirm your existing beliefs.

REACTANCE
You'd rather do the opposite of what someone is trying to make you do.

SUNK COST FALLACY
You irrationally cling to things that have already cost you something.

DUNNING KREUGER EFFECT
The more you know, the less confident you are likely to be.

BACKFIRE EFFECT
When your core beliefs are challenged, it can cause you to believe in them more strongly.

DECLINISM
You remember the past better than it was, and expect the future to be worse than it will likely be.

FRAMING EFFECT
You allow yourself to be influenced by context and delivery.

NEGATIVITY BIAS
You allow negative things to disproportionally influence your thinking.

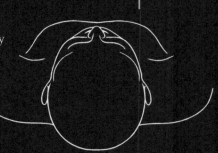

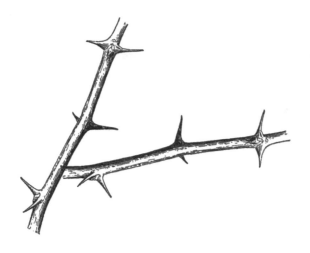

How to do Shadow Work

Shadow work involves exploring these unconscious aspects of ourselves in a safe and controlled environment. This can include journaling, meditation, therapy, or working with a spiritual teacher or guide (**The Shadow Work Journal** can serve as your guide). The goal of shadow work is to bring the unconscious into consciousness and integrate it into our lives. By doing this, we can gain a greater understanding of our motivations, reactions, and behaviors, and make changes to live more authentic lives. We all have multiple parts to ourselves, and if we don't embrace the entirety of our being, we wouldn't be able to live a whole and authentic life. The process of integrating the shadow leads to self-acceptance, forgiveness, and unconditional love.

In order to flush out your shadow, you must be willing to **catch yourself** in moments of negativity and question where it stems from. Use this journal's **"Getting to the Root of your Shadow"** pages when you notice yourself becoming irritated, anxious, angry, or sad. When facing your shadow, it is important to take small positive actions that improve your physical and mental well-being. Drink more water than you think you need, dress up more, shower, cleanse your face, eat something light and healthy, do breathing exercises, or listen to music you enjoy. Know that the discomfort will pass and you will feel like yourself again.

> *"Knowing your own darkness is the best method for dealing with the darknesses of other people."*
>
> ## -CARL JUNG

The shadow carries all the things we do not want to know about ourselves or do not like. While difficult and painful, it is important that we work at owning our shadow to bring it into a relationship with our consciousness. Owning up to our shadow is an important part of self-awareness and healing. As you go through **The Shadow Work Journal,** remember to show those parts of yourself, unconditional love.

The Mindset: Self-Compassion

One of the key aspects of shadow work is self-compassion. When we begin to explore the shadow, it can be challenging to face the parts of ourselves that we reject or hide. It is important to approach shadow work with a non-judgmental attitude and to treat yourself with the same kindness and compassion that you would offer a friend. By doing this, you can create a safe and supportive environment for exploration and growth. Self-compassion involves recognizing and accepting our own human limitations, failures, and experiences of suffering, rather than harsh self-criticism and judgment.

Our culture often emphasizes perfectionism and individual achievement, which can lead to feelings of inadequacy and self-criticism when we fall short.

Self-compassion is the foundation of a meaningful life, for it is only through the lens of kindness and understanding towards ourselves that we can truly see and accept others.

The Importance of Grounding

Another important aspect of shadow work is grounding. Shadow work can be intense and emotionally challenging, and it is important to take steps to ensure that you are in a safe and stable state of mind before and after the process. This can include meditation, deep breathing, or other practices that help you feel centered and grounded. Whenever you need it, flip to the grounding technique page found later in this journal. Grounding is a technique that helps to anchor us in the present moment, to connect with our bodies, and to find stability and balance in a chaotic world. Grounding is about being fully present in the moment and in our bodies. It helps to reduce stress and anxiety by bringing us out of our heads and into the present moment.

Grounding can also help to increase focus and concentration.

It is important to ground yourself before and after using **The Shadow Work Journal.**

Here are a few ways to easily ground yourself:

1. Simple Recognition: Recognize common humanity: Remember that everyone experiences setbacks, failures, and moments of suffering. You are not alone, and your experiences are a normal part of the human experience.

2. Self-care: Engage in activities that bring you joy, relaxation, and a sense of well-being. This can include things like exercise, hobbies, spending time with loved ones, and getting enough sleep.

3. Affirmations: Using positive affirmations can help to reduce stress and increase feelings of well-being.

4. Sensory stimulation: Engaging our senses through activities such as walking in nature, smelling essential oils, or eating a nourishing meal can help to bring us into the present moment.

5. Deep breathing: Taking slow, deep breaths can help to calm the mind and reduce stress.

How to Spot your Shadow-Self

Spotting your shadow-self often begins with noticing your triggers, recognizing patterns in your behavior and life experiences, and understanding your projections.

1. Noticing Your Triggers:
Triggers are emotional responses that are often intense and seemingly disproportionate to the situation at hand. They are indicators that a part of you, often a shadow aspect, feels threatened or hurt. When you're triggered, it can feel as if you're reacting automatically, without a conscious choice. These triggers are valuable clues, pointing towards your underlying unresolved issues or 'shadows'. To spot your triggers, take a step back and objectively look at situations that cause you to react intensely. Is there a common theme or factor? It could be a word, an action, a type of person, or even a place that repeatedly causes an emotional upheaval in you.

2. Recognizing Patterns:
Patterns are repetitive behaviors that may not serve you but seem hard to break free from. They often manifest in your relationships, choices, reactions, or habits. These patterns can be a sign of a shadow self that's trying to make its presence felt. Recognizing these patterns involves self-reflection. Consider the common threads in your past experiences, relationships, and reactions. Are you repeatedly drawn to similar types of relationships or situations, only to experience the same outcomes? Do you often react in the same way, even when you wish you didn't? These repetitive patterns might indicate areas where shadow work can be beneficial.

3. Understanding Projections:

Projections are aspects of ourselves that we unconsciously place onto others. These can be qualities that we both admire and detest. When we have a strong emotional reaction to someone else's behavior or qualities, it often signifies a disowned part of ourselves – a shadow aspect.

To understand your projections, consider the characteristics in others that you find extremely irritating or, conversely, overly admire. Then, ask yourself if these traits could be parts of yourself that you've disowned or idealized.

4. Pay Attention to Dreams:

Your dreams are a rich source of symbolism and unconscious vault. Try to recall and record your dreams upon waking up. Analyze the symbols, emotions, and themes present in your dreams. They can provide valuable insights into your shadows, fears, desires, and unexpressed parts of yourself.

5. Explore Childhood and Past Experiences:

Reflect on your childhood, family dynamics, and significant life events. Identify any unresolved issues, traumas, or unmet needs that might have contributed to the development of your shadows. Exploring these experiences with compassion and curiosity can lead to profound healing and integration.

Integrating your Shadow-Self

Emotional Freedom Techniques (EFT) tapping is a powerful therapeutic tool that combines elements of cognitive therapy and acupressure. It can be a valuable method for integrating your shadow self and facilitating deep emotional healing. By combining specific tapping sequences on meridian points with focused attention on unresolved emotions and beliefs, EFT can help release energetic blockages, promote self-acceptance, and facilitate the integration of shadow aspects. In this guide, we will explore how to use EFT tapping as a means of integrating your shadow self and promoting holistic healing.

Identify the shadow aspects you wish to integrate. Reflect on the emotions, beliefs, or memories that arise when you think about these aspects. Learn the Basic Tapping Points: Familiarize yourself with the basic tapping points used in EFT. These points include the top of the head, eyebrow, side of the eye, under the eye, under the nose, chin, collarbone, and under the arm. Gently tap each point with two or three fingers while repeating a relevant statement or focusing on the associated emotion.

Another technique is to use inner-child affirmations. Craft affirmations that specifically address the shadows you have identified. Affirmations should be positive, present tense statements that reflect self-acceptance, healing, and integration.

Ongoing awareness is a powerful tool for integrating shadows and promoting personal growth. By becoming a "butterfly net" for your triggers and negative thoughts, you can actively engage in the process of identifying, understanding, and integrating your shadows. This practice cultivates self-awareness, empowers you to respond consciously, and opens the door to transformation and healing.

Emotional Triggers

Shame: Shame is an intense emotion that arises when you believe there is something fundamentally wrong with who you are. It is a deeply painful and isolating experience that can stem from feeling unworthy, inadequate, or humiliated. Shame can manifest as a heavy burden that weighs us down, making us feel small and undeserving of love and acceptance. It often arises from societal expectations, past traumas, or internalized beliefs. Overcoming shame requires compassion, self-acceptance, and a recognition of our inherent worthiness as human beings.

Guilt: Guilt arises when we believe we have done something wrong or violated our own moral code. It's a form of self-condemnation and blame, mixed with a sense of regret. Guilt can be a constructive emotion, because it reveals your values and helps you learn from mistakes. It signals a need for accountability and encourages us to make amends or change our behavior.

Anger: Anger is a powerful and complex emotion that spurs in response to perceived threats, injustice, or frustration. It can range from mild to intense and can manifest as a physical and emotional response. Anger is a natural and valid emotion that reveals a need for change or boundaries. Uncontrolled or excessive anger can lead to destructive behavior and harm to oneself and others.

Sadness: Sadness is a deep and poignant emotion that arises in response to loss, disappointment, or unfulfilled desires. Sadness can be triggered by a variety of experiences, such as the loss of a loved one, the end of a relationship, or unmet expectations. It is a natural and necessary part of the human experience.

Embarrassment: This emotion stems from feeling self-conscious, awkward, or humiliated in social situations. It often happens when you think you have violated social norms. Ongoing embarrassment can lead to feeling shame and a desire to hide.

Jealousy: Jealousy is a cover-up emotion. It masks itself as anger or judgement, when underneath it's sadness and dissatisfaction of self. It can lead you to compare yourself to others, and protect what you have.

Regret: Regret occurs when you feel sadness over past actions or decisions. The truth is that most people regret what they did *not* do more than they regret what they did do.

Fear: Fear is a primal and powerful emotion that arises in response to perceived threats or dangers. It triggers a domino of physiological and emotional responses to keep you "safe". Fear can serve as a protective mechanism, but irrational fear can limit our experiences and growth. Overcoming fear involves understanding its root causes, challenging irrational beliefs, and gradually exposing yourself to feared situations in a safe and supportive manner.

"The journey of self-discovery requires the willingness to explore the depths of our shadows and the heights of our potential."

UNLESS WE DO CONSCIOUS WORK ON IT,
THE SHADOW IS ALMOST ALWAYS
PROJECTED: THAT IS, IT IS NEATLY LAID
ON SOMEONE OR SOMETHING ELSE
SO WE DO NOT HAVE TO TAKE
RESPONSIBILITY FOR IT.

ROBERT JOHNSON

———

UNCONSCIOUS

Habits + Patterns

Emotions

Protection

Controls Bodily Functions

Belief

Desires

Blaming, denying, lying

Attachment to things, thoughts, feelings

CONSCIOUS

Logic

Filter

Analytical

Movement

Decision Making

Short-term Memory

Will Power

Critical Thinking

2

SHADOW WORK
ACTIVITIES

SHADOW WORK ACTIVITIES

It takes time to train yourself to identify where your shadows arise. Taking 5-10 minutes to practice a shadow work activity is a great way to intentionally reflect on your relationships, reactions, and inner dialogue.

Doing these activities and reflections might make you uncomfortable or squirmy- but that is part of the process. Use this section to record your discoveries and insights and look back on them later to remember the traits of your shadow.

You may complete the shadow work activities at your own pace, and in your own order.

Wound Mapping

EXERCISE:

Identify your inner-child wound based on the attributes listed on the next page. Abandonment, guilt, trust, and neglect are the four major kinds of inner child wounds. You may find one or more that align with your persona.

WHY:

It hurts to be offended or harmed, especially at a young age. This is an exercise that allows you to pinpoint emotional wounds from your early childhood. These wounds are what cause certain behaviors and habitual thoughts that do not serve us. By identifying your inner-child wound, you will hold more space for compassion towards your humanness, and provide a healthy foundation to begin your shadow work journey.

ABANDONMENT WOUND

- Feels "left out"
- Fears being left
- Hates being alone
- Co-dependent
- Threatens to leave
- Normally attracts emotionally unavailable people

GUILT WOUND

- Feels "sorry" or "bad"
- Doesn't like to ask for things
- Uses guilt to manipulate
- Is afraid to set boundaries
- Normally attracts people who make them feel guilty

TRUST WOUND

- Is afraid to be hurt
- Doesn't trust themselves
- Finds ways to not trust people
- Feels insecure and needs lots of external validation
- Doesn't feel safe
- Normally attracts people who don't feel safe

NEGLECT WOUND

- Struggles to let things go
- Has low self-worth
- Gets angry easily
- Struggles to say "no"
- Represses emotions
- Fears being vulnerable
- Normally attracts people who don't appreciate them or make them feel seen.

Fill in the _____

EXERCISE:

Fill in the blank! Read through the paragraph and fill in the blanks without hesitation. If you can't come up with a word, try looking at your surroundings, find an object and think of word associations for that object.

WHY:

Your mind naturally makes uninhibited connections through selective words and word associations. Because shadows lie beneath the conscious mind, you will be surprised to reveal raw emotions and beliefs from your subconscious from this exercise.

Reflection Questions

What memories did I extract from this exercise?

How can I reframe these memories so that they don't
continue to hurt and hinder me in the future?

How can I regularly serve myself with compassionate
consolation, as I would give to my child-self?

ou

part 3

Fill in the Blank

_____ scares me the

most. When I become scared or anxious, I tend to

_____. It sometimes sucks

because _____

_____ and this makes me

feel _____ . My anxiety teaches me

that _____ and_____.

I understand that I am _____

but I love myself unconditionally.

Reflection Questions

What is my current fear and if it were to happen,
what would be the best-case scenario?

If my fears and anxieties were teachers, what lessons
would they teach me?

How can I build a more positive outlook on the
unknown future?

part 4

Fill in the Blank

_____ makes me tense.

I typically feel this tense sensation in my_____

_____ . This makes me very _____

_____. When this happens, I start to

_____ . I think it is because _____

and_____ . Next time I feel tense, I

will soothe myself by_____ .

Reflection Questions

When does my anxiety take over my mind and body?
Do I see a common recurring theme as to what triggers my anxiety?

What can I physically do to release my
anxious energy and tension?

What thoughts help soothe my anxiety? How can I improve my
self-talk to be less self-critical when these emotions arise?

part 5

Fill in the Blank

As a child, I was reprimanded for _____

_____. My response was to

_____ and _____ . After this,

I've always been _____ .

I care so much about_____ and

_____ . It triggers me now when

_____ .

I now hold a compassionate space for my full self

and embrace this part of me.

Reflection Questions

In what ways have I been reprimanded in my
childhood and beyond?

How did this impact what I choose to do/not do in the
present moment? In what ways am I holding back because
of these experiences?

What activities can I partake in to fuel my inner-child and
allow him/her to feel fully expressive?

part 6

Fill in the Blank

As I grow older, I feel like the _____ part

of me becomes further and further away. I feel

_____ towards this. Sometimes I put

myself in a box by_____ .

I understand that I am ever-changing and evolving

each day. One way I can foster my child-self is by

_____ and _____ . I will

always recognize the_____ part of

me and show that version of myself love and

recognition.

Reflection Questions

What do I admire about my past-self that I wish I could
continue to foster more in the present day?

When/Where do I find myself hiding parts of my
personality in order to fit the mold?

What do I think will happen if I were to be my full self
during these instances?

Release Stagnant Energy

EXERCISE:

Release trapped stagnant energy by choosing one of the following activities on the next page. Become aware of how you feel both before and after your exercise is complete.

WHY:

Everything is energy in a world of both the physical and the metaphysical. When you feel "off" this means there is negative energy trapped in your body. Stagnant energy causes you to feel irritated and imbalanced. Many times, stagnant energy will manifest itself in the form of pain or tension in the body. Doing simple actions such as dancing, going on a walk, and meditating will help restore balance and unleash lingering stagnant energy stored within the body.

Touch the Earth

Stretch

Draw or Doodle

Put on a song you
love and dance.

Write a Poem

Make Art

Do a Gratitude
Meditation

Bathe in Sunlight
for 10 Min

Go for a Walk

Take a shower. Envision the water
washing away lingering negative
energy.

Inner Child Affirmations

EXERCISE:

Find a mirror and repeat the following inner-child affirmations out loud to yourself. Repeat the affirmations multiple times and notice how it begins to feel more natural and part of your inner truth.

WHY:

An affirmation is a positive phrase or statement that you can repeat to yourself on a daily or weekly cadence. By using affirmations, you can reprogram your mind to spotlight positive emotions and beliefs that may help you recover from negative self-narratives, suffering, and unhealthy habits. Once repeated enough times, an affirmation will embed into your inner consciousness- shifting old limiting thought patterns and unlocking new beliefs that help you reach your full potential. You can change the way you think, which will change the way you act, and become the person you want to be.

Inner Child Affirmations

- ✦ I release the feeling of guilt, hurt, and shame

- ✦ I am protected

- ✦ I accept every aspect of myself and my personality

- ✦ I am loved

- ✦ I am capable of every dream and worthy of every desire

- ✦ I dream big

- ✦ I am safe

- ✦ I am beautiful and I accept myself for who I am.

- ✦ I honor the child within me

- ✦ I show myself compassion

- ✦ I am so much more than I thought I could be

- ✦ My needs and feelings are valid

- ✦ I deserve happiness

- ✦ A feeling of peace comforts me

- ✦ I am in control of my feelings

- ✦ No one can inflict anything on me that I cannot handle

- ✦ I love myself

- ✦ I can protect myself

- ✦ Setting firm boundaries comes easy for me

- ✦ My energy is limitless

Gratitude List

EXERCISE:

Take 5 minutes to create a gratitude list. Think of all the things that bring you health, peace, and love. List both big and small things in life, from your home appliances to your relationships with others. If it feels right, acknowledge the things that brought you pain in the past but have taught you patience and healing. When your list is complete, take a moment to say "*thank you*" to each one for existing and making you who you are.

WHY:

Neuroscientist Dr. Rick Hanson suggests that the brain takes the shape of the state of mind we rest upon. If we rest upon doubt, sadness, irritability, it may bring more anger, anxiety, and depression into our lives. And if we rest upon joy, contentment, and love, we may bring more abundance, and peace into our lives. Gratitude is a wonderful way of improving your life and creating more abundance by appreciating what you currently have.

Gratitude List

- ♥ _____
- ♥ _____
- ♥ _____
- ♥ _____
- ♥ _____
- ♥ _____
- ♥ _____
- ♥ _____
- ♥ _____
- ♥ _____
- ♥ _____
- ♥ _____

A Letter to Yourself

EXERCISE:

Find some time to take a step back from your normal routine and do a deep reflection. Think back to a difficulty you faced in the past, and write a letter addressed to that version of yourself. Write your letter with love and empathy. Share the advice you needed to hear. The content of your letter should be unique to your experience. Start with one sentence and see where your heart flows.

WHY:

Writing a letter to your past self is therapeutic and will help you gain closure, clarity, and inner peace. Your inner child is still inside of you, waiting to be heard and nurtured. You may even find that this letter may resonate with you in the future.

A Letter to Yourself

_____

_____

_____

_____

_____

_____

_____

_____

_____

_____

_____

_____

_____

_____

_____

_____

_____

_____

_____

_____

_____

_____

_____

Mirror-Gazing

EXERCISE:

Find a mirror that you can sit down in front of. Take a seat and get close up to the mirror so that you can gaze into your eyes. Spend 5-10 minutes looking directly into your eyes, and try your best not to look away. If you feel comfortable, talk to your reflection and have a conversation with your shadow. When you are done, tell yourself that you are safe and loved.

WHY:

Mirror gazing is an intimate way to face your deepest fears and insecurities. During mirror-gazing, you may begin to see aspects of yourself that repulse you. You may come across thoughts, doubts, and fears that keep you from experiencing peace. You may even see physical parts of yourself shifting. This exercise will allow you to mentally wrestle with yourself and surrender. Do not be afraid, and show yourself compassion every second.

Mirror-Gazing

Find a mirror and sit in front of it closely.
Spend 5-10 minutes gazing at yourself. Try your best not to look away.
Talk to your reflection as if it were your shadow self.
Afterward, answer the reflective questions below:

What recurring thoughts did I have?_____

What emotions arose?_____

How do I feel now? _____

_____

What conversations did I have? What breakthroughs did I discover?

Fill in the Box

EXERCISE:

Read the prompts below and respond by filling each box provided with your authentic answer.

WHY:

You are shaped by your experiences. Reflective writing prompts will guide you towards understanding who you are and why. This will help you recognize patterns and habits that shape you.

Fill in the Box

Do I feel guilty if I put my
needs first?

How important is my
own happiness?

In what ways do I show
love to myself?

I think I still need
to work on....

3

SHADOW WORK
JOURNAL PROMPTS

JOURNAL PROMPTS

Journaling is such a powerful tool to unravel your emotions and beliefs. Writing about your experiences helps you become more aware, intuitive, and present. For as little as 10 minutes per day, journaling can change the way you behave and think.

Use these shadow work journaling prompts to lean into your unconscious mind and build an understanding of your shadow. Please note that these journaling prompts get deep and dark, but do not let that hold you back.

Fear

Imagine yourself unafraid. You have no doubts, no worries, no fears of the unknown. The things you used to worry about do not exist. Write about what you would do if this was the case. What would you do if you weren't afraid?

Putting Yourself Last

Where are you putting yourself last? Think of the last time you did this to yourself in an unhealthy way. Why did you put aside your own well-being and needs?

Inspiration

Think of a time when you felt a spark of joy and inspiration.
Your mind was full of awe and wonder. Where were you?
What were you doing? Were you with someone?
Write about what inspires you.

Jealousy

Who are you jealous of? What desires lie behind your
jealousy? How often do you feel jealousy?

Tolerating

What are you tolerating that you do not want to be? Think of any self sabotaging behaviors and question why you continue to repeat those negative actions and/or thoughts.

Dream Life

Envision your dream life. What would your daily experience be if you were living your dream life tomorrow? What is holding you back from experiencing this?

Facing Your Fear

What is your biggest fear in life? If it were to happen, what would you do? How would you feel?

Parental Influence

What parts of your parents or guardians do you notice reflected in yourself? What traits, both good and bad, are you inheriting from them? How can you break the negative behavioral chains that run through your family?

Low Energy

Think back to the last time you were drained.
What were you doing? Who were you with?
What did you need at that moment?

Judgment

What do you judge others for? Do you do the same things that you judge others for? What do you judge yourself for?

Holding on

What are you holding onto that still hurts you so deeply?

Avoidance

Motivation moves you forward, but what are you moving away
from? What do you try your best to avoid in life? Are there
certain emotions attached to these things that you don't want
to experience?

Childhood

In your childhood, what did you not receive? How has this impacted you? What do you think would be different if you had received this?

Self

Your authentic self is what hides behind layers of learned masks. Is there anything you wish more people knew about you? Why don't they know already?

Secret

What is your biggest secret? Why is this a secret? How would you feel if others knew?

Anger

What makes you angry? Why does it make you angry? How do you cope with your anger?

Change

Change is a natural constant. Sometimes, change is optional.
Do you prefer change or do you avoid it? Why? How well do
you handle change?

Anxiety

What makes you anxious? Why does it make you anxious?
How do you cope with anxiety?

Less

Reflect on everything you have, both physical and nonphysical. Sometimes things can energetically weigh our quality of living down. What do you need less of?

Traits

What traits do you dislike the most about yourself? How can you show these parts of yourself compassion and love?

Nightmare

What is your worst nightmare?
Why is this your worst nightmare?

Pride

Reflect on your past accomplishments in life: personal, physical, academic, spiritual, social, or other. Out of all of them, what are you most proud of? Why are you most proud of this? How does this motivate you currently?

Self Image

How do you think others see you? How would you like to be seen and why? What do you believe is the most authentic version of yourself?

Childhood Trauma

What experiences did you have as a child that impacted you in a negative way? Why was it so traumatic?

Identify Your Fear

What is fear to you? What makes you afraid? Instead of writing "I am afraid of..." phrase it as "I experience fear when...". This will allow you to break the habit of identifying fear as part of yourself.

Personal Change

What are 10 ways you have changed in the past 10 years? Are these mainly positive or negative?

Biggest Dreams

What are your biggest dreams in life? If your biggest dream happened, what would you do? How would you feel?

Freedom

What does freedom mean to you? When do you feel free?
What is stopping you from experiencing freedom?

Critical

When are you the hardest on yourself? Why is that? How do you feel when you become hyper critical? In what ways can you be more kind and understanding?

4

**GET TO THE ROOT
OF YOUR SHADOW**

GETTING TO THE ROOT OF YOUR SHADOW

Come to this section whenever you are facing your shadow in real-time.

Behaviors of your unconscious shadow include:

- Feeling angry, irritated, or anxious without a clear reason.

- Blaming external factors for your problems, consistently playing the victim.

- Ongoing negative thoughts and laziness.

- Lack of motivation and doubtfulness of one's capabilities.

- Jealousy, negative thoughts towards others.

- Feelings of guilt, shame.

EXAMPLE

Getting to the root of your shadow

Find a dim, quiet space to sit in. Tune into your shadow.

What is triggering my shadow? *My job and presentation tomorrow*

What thoughts am I having? *I want to quit. This job sucks life from me. I can't do this presentation tomorrow, I don't feel prepared...*

What emotions am I experiencing?

Anxiety, fear

Close your eyes. Listen to your inner voice.
What 3 words come to your mind? Write them down. They hold meaning.

Trapped	*Nervous*	*Heavy*

What memories or images come to mind when you focus on these words?
Connect with your inner child.

I think of a bird in a cage looking out from the inside. I know that freedom exists on the other side, but i'm nervous to fly. I'm nervous and anxious about my capabilities- what if I can't go far if I leave? I feel heavy, and like something is weighing me down. I felt like this as a child in school, always looking outside the window, and struggling to understand the material in class.

Set the intention to energetically accept & love your inner child. Let go.

Getting to the root of your shadow

Find a dim, quiet space to sit in. Tune into your shadow.

What is triggering my shadow? _____

What thoughts am I having? _____

_____

What emotions am I experiencing?

_____

Close your eyes. Listen to your inner voice.
What 3 words come to your mind? Write them down. They hold meaning.

What memories or images come to mind when you focus on these words?
Connect with your inner child.

_____

_____

_____

_____

_____

_____

Set the intention to energetically accept & love your inner child. Let go.

Getting to the root of your shadow

Find a dim, quiet space to sit in. Tune into your shadow.

What is triggering my shadow? _____

What thoughts am I having? _____

_____

What emotions am I experiencing?

_____

Close your eyes. Listen to your inner voice.
What 3 words come to your mind? Write them down. They hold meaning.

What memories or images come to mind when you focus on these words?
Connect with your inner child.

_____

_____

_____

_____

_____

_____

Set the intention to energetically accept & love your inner child. Let go.

Getting to the root of your shadow

Find a dim, quiet space to sit in. Tune into your shadow.

What is triggering my shadow? _____

What thoughts am I having? _____

_____

What emotions am I experiencing?

_____

Close your eyes. Listen to your inner voice.
What 3 words come to your mind? Write them down. They hold meaning.

What memories or images come to mind when you focus on these words?
Connect with your inner child.

_____

_____

_____

_____

_____

_____

Set the intention to energetically accept & love your inner child. Let go.

Getting to the root of your shadow

Find a dim, quiet space to sit in. Tune into your shadow.

What is triggering my shadow? _____

What thoughts am I having? _____

_____

What emotions am I experiencing?

_____

Close your eyes. Listen to your inner voice.
What 3 words come to your mind? Write them down. They hold meaning.

What memories or images come to mind when you focus on these words?
Connect with your inner child.

_____

_____

_____

_____

_____

_____

Set the intention to energetically accept & love your inner child. Let go.

Getting to the root of your shadow

Find a dim, quiet space to sit in. Tune into your shadow.

What is triggering my shadow? _____

What thoughts am I having? _____

_____

What emotions am I experiencing?

_____

Close your eyes. Listen to your inner voice.
What 3 words come to your mind? Write them down. They hold meaning.

What memories or images come to mind when you focus on these words?
Connect with your inner child.

_____

_____

_____

_____

_____

_____

Set the intention to energetically accept & love your inner child. Let go.

Getting to the root of your shadow

Find a dim, quiet space to sit in. Tune into your shadow.

What is triggering my shadow? _____

What thoughts am I having? _____

_____

What emotions am I experiencing?

_____

Close your eyes. Listen to your inner voice.
What 3 words come to your mind? Write them down. They hold meaning.

What memories or images come to mind when you focus on these words?
Connect with your inner child.

_____

_____

_____

_____

_____

_____

Set the intention to energetically accept & love your inner child. Let go.

Getting to the root of your shadow

Find a dim, quiet space to sit in. Tune into your shadow.

What is triggering my shadow? _____

What thoughts am I having? _____

_____

What emotions am I experiencing?

_____

Close your eyes. Listen to your inner voice.
What 3 words come to your mind? Write them down. They hold meaning.

What memories or images come to mind when you focus on these words?
Connect with your inner child.

_____

_____

_____

_____

_____

_____

Set the intention to energetically accept & love your inner child. Let go.

Getting to the root of your shadow

Find a dim, quiet space to sit in. Tune into your shadow.

What is triggering my shadow? _____

What thoughts am I having? _____

_____

What emotions am I experiencing?

_____

Close your eyes. Listen to your inner voice.
What 3 words come to your mind? Write them down. They hold meaning.

What memories or images come to mind when you focus on these words?
Connect with your inner child.

_____

_____

_____

_____

_____

_____

Set the intention to energetically accept & love your inner child. Let go.

Getting to the root of your shadow

Find a dim, quiet space to sit in. Tune into your shadow.

What is triggering my shadow? _____

What thoughts am I having? _____

_____

What emotions am I experiencing?

_____

Close your eyes. Listen to your inner voice.
What 3 words come to your mind? Write them down. They hold meaning.

What memories or images come to mind when you focus on these words?
Connect with your inner child.

_____

_____

_____

_____

_____

_____

Set the intention to energetically accept & love your inner child. Let go.

Getting to the root of your shadow

Find a dim, quiet space to sit in. Tune into your shadow.

What is triggering my shadow? _____

What thoughts am I having? _____

_____

What emotions am I experiencing?

_____

Close your eyes. Listen to your inner voice.
What 3 words come to your mind? Write them down. They hold meaning.

What memories or images come to mind when you focus on these words?
Connect with your inner child.

_____

_____

_____

_____

_____

_____

Set the intention to energetically accept & love your inner child. Let go.

Resources

- National Institute of Mental Health (NIMH) - This is a government-funded organization that provides information and resources on various mental health conditions.

- American Psychological Association (APA) - This is a professional organization for psychologists that offers information and resources for both mental health professionals and the general public.

- Psychology Today (Psychologytoday.com/us) - This is a directory website that allows you to search by location and provider type for therapists, psychologists, and more.

- Zenfulnote App - This is an app that allows you to track emotional triggers and moods. It is a virtual space for self-exploration with prompts, exercises and learning materials around self-healing and shadow work.

- National Alliance on Mental Illness (NAMI) - This is a grassroots organization that provides support, education, and advocacy for people living with mental health conditions.

- Depression and Bipolar Support Alliance (DBSA) - This is a national organization that provides peer support, education, and advocacy for people living with depression and bipolar disorder.

- The Depression Project - This is an online platform that provides resources, support, and a community for people living with depression.

- Therapy for Black Girls - This is an online directory and resource that helps black women with support from licensed mental health providers.

- Therapy for LatinX - This is a database of therapists who either identify as LatinX or have worked closely with LatinX communities and understands their needs. www.therapyforlatinx.com

- Talkspace - This is an online therapy platform that provides therapy for people experiencing depression and other mental health conditions.

- BetterHelp - This is an online therapy platform that provides therapy for people experiencing depression and other mental health conditions.

- ADAA - This is a US-based nonprofit organization that provides education, support, and advocacy for people living with anxiety, depression, and other related disorders.

WE'RE HERE BECAUSE OF YOU.

When you're supporting our business, you're
supporting a dream.

Share a picture or video of your journal on TikTok or
Instagram for **20% OFF your next purchase!**

DM @zenfulnote or email keila@zenfulnote.com with
your video link to receive your special discount.

Let's vibe!

Learn about The 369 Method, Manifesting
Techniques, Shadow Work, and more. Follow
our @zenfulnote social channels.